MEDITATIONS

Stefania Rotariu

*Keep your foot from falling
and your heart
from punishing itself...*

Published by Dolman Scott in 2024

ISBN:
PoD: 978-1-915351-29-6
eBook: 978-1-915351-30-2

DolmanScott
www.dolmanscott.com

AGING

Old age does not mean just the passing of the body into powerlessness...

This word is deep and heavy as meaning, understood only by those who love people and are able to devote themselves to them. The wise human knows the definition of old age, as to be a wisdom. He knows that every hair from the human head is a memory, of everything that human has been through in life in his journey.

To be human, is a big thing...

The old age seen by people brings loneliness, few friends around and daily habits. Old age seen by the Creator is like a favour given to his creation called man; a great blessing to see your children grown up, householders in their homes and with grandchildren.

To be old with grey hair,
Which flows in many waves
And don't to pass from the earth,
Without the dreams, ideals...

To be old with
grey hair...

When a human grows old gracefully, in the same time with the passage of years, it feels its being bathed in the light of wisdom. And that man look for the truth, dignity, purity of soul, patience, forgiveness, courage, purification of sins, kindness, gentleness, honesty, care, continuous love, stability, closeness to divinity, giving, the reconciliation with one-self. And when iniquity looking for him, he knows how to chase it away.

The state of the wise human...

Thus the wise human's face becomes beautiful, in the state in which God left it. With the silver hair that signifying accumulated experience during life. With a chosen character, which strongly conveys to those around the feeling of firmness in making good decisions and a shoulder as support to the ones who are in trouble. It is the tireless counselor, who awaits anyone seeks wise counsel.

Those who don't have elders, let them buy from those who do...

The human who has gone through life, will always have an answer to some questions. Answers that were won due to the experience accumulated over the years, the material and moral riches left by those before it and the education it acquired throughout its life.

The beaten path, is the shortest path...

The advice of the elders comes like a spring with cold water, to saturate the hearts of those thirsty for love.

The educated and wise human gathers up the advice of elders as the precious treasures, while all the prompting and good habits are their roads to success, which it will give in exchange, when the time of trouble comes.

Old age, rare coat, if I could to make you lighter...

The people without culture, character, compassion, proper education, logical thinking, soul joy, humanity, intelligence, kindness, they treat old age as a disease which attribute to the elderly.

If the youth were a flower,
Even she would wither,
When old age looking for her,
As the sun in the fields...

These condemned to eternity keep the elderly at bay, often abandoning and disregarding them. They do not fulfill their family role, in their lives. Some use the elderly for personal interests and then abandon them, naming them useless people. All people should know that lives are received from God and that these cannot be taken by anyone, except the one who gave them.

No one decides of human's years...

No one received life in any other way to be master of it, nor the right to count the years how long to live or when to die. No matter how rich would be, poor, skilled or unskillful, all humans die and go to the same place.

The education is sacred...

People should not force themselves to live according to the dictates of this world, which day by day they lose its definition of humanity. It would be better if they were guided by the sound education, that they inherited from their parents and their grandparents. Let each person live its life in peace, without making the lives of others difficult, because it is not known when the hour of his departure from this world will ring. And if there is sadness after that human, then it will be known that it was a good human, because there is no human who does not grow old or to remain immortal.

When you are young, you have no way of knowing how hard old age is...

When you're young, your house is full of children, your table is with everything, friends, neighbors, worries, problems, joys, you are overwhelmed by everything and tired. But, when you get older your house becomes empty, your table no longer has to be full, friends disappear, you don't know your neighbors anymore, worries and the problems become less, joys become rare and less, you not longer busy and tired of anyone's presence. Therefore, care should be taken in youth with who we get close to, what kind of people are around, so that we can enjoy the old years together.

BETRAYAL

Betraying the country, is the greatest sin…

The great fighter for justice, Petre Țuțea (1902-1991) said about foreigners that: "We took the Halloween from them..." and that: "they took from us the gold, oil, wood, gases, deposits, waters and the lands...", calling us a "a people of idiots..."

And rightfully so, if we look at what we gave to them and what we got from them in return, Petre Țuțea was kind of right.

What you don't like, don't do to another...

Only the human who is full on the outside and empty on the inside, betrays.

Why should a human betray another?

When you put your hand in the fire for someone, you will burn yourself. And when you vouch for someone, need to know that it is one of the first people who will betray you, when needed.

If someone is not ready for a relationship or a commitment, it's better to leave than to ruin. That way it can produce less suffering, hatred, hopelessness and disappointment. Also, when a human has stretched out a helping hand to you, kiss it, instead of betraying it, and biting it with the mouth of sin. The weak human always betrays, because it is unable to rise to the level, of his benefactor.

Fear of responsibility leads to betrayal and hiding the truth…

If someone want to make a new move, then to be decided and do it, however justified or unjustified it is in doing it. Because that move can be the solution to his life and whom it wants to betray. This is how himself will save staying away from betrayal, the lying and hiding the facts, following that things will be resolved in the truth without lies and hiding.

Avoid the person which tells you nice words, but without fulfilling them...

Many times, the gilded mouth is the most sinful trap and through coverage, a human is betrayed and manipulated.

Better to be confronted than to be betrayed...

If things are told straight to your face, then the purpose of that discussion is to make the progress, to learn the truth and to know that you are not being betrayed.

Who hides the truth, gives reason to betrayal...

When a human does not like to be told the truth, then is a two-faced human who works his tricks in secret. The righteous human will always be direct and open to the truth, even if the truth hurts and causes many upsets. Is better a human to keep its heart pure than to betray secretly, and the justice to be his pillow of rest.

Who has two parallel lives, will be lose one...

Can't be build two lives, two families, two secrets at the same time, because you can't split yourself into two parts at the same time and the time will come when you should give an account to one of the parties. And then you will have to choose, and it is possible to make a choice by the spur of the moment, which may be the choice of your destruction.

You cannot make happy two families…

You cannot make happy two families at the same time, on this earth. God gave only one family on earth consisting of woman, man and children. Who have several families must be able to carry all the weight in his back, as a slave sold to the work and well-being of the women it serves.

Betrayers in relationships are the people of lies...

Whoever betrays in a relationship is a weak human, a human who has no dignity and from whom you must run as far as possible, because how many times he will lie that it is honest, so many times it will betray. Treason and lies are written, in the blood of these people. They cannot live in the truth nor change, no matter how many chances would receive. On the contrary, receiving chances, confidence in them grows and they believe themselves victorious punishing kindness.

The traitor's not worth trust...

No traitor deserves to have a chosen soul by its side. The sacrifice and punishment would be very great and without any thanks for the sacrificed person.

Lie is equal with the betrayal...

Eyes kept down and angry words thrown to the wind just to end a discussion, do not prove that the storm will soon pass. At some point everything will become clear, and the one who is wronged will seek the justice and only then will the misunderstandings be resolved.

Experiences

I accompanied myself with the pain,
She was my friend on the earth,
And I thought that she is the meaning,
Of the forgiving human and the holy human.

Then I accompanied the sadness,
I believed that my tearful eyes,
They will cover the gentleness,
With her love and nature.

But trouble didn't bypass me either
And always he broke from me,
Many times filling my cheek,
With bitter tears and sighs.

And when the power came,
To master them all,
Not to tire myself of anything
And no tears to start again.

I got up, as if out of sin,
Wiping my cheek with my hand,
Thinking that my dear father,
Will send help to get over my trouble.

CHARACTER

Character is wealth of a human, it is inherited or formed throughout life, it having influences from the past and the contemporary generations.

There was a time when people, there were people...

Our grandparents said that a good human is known by its face and a tree by its fruit. The passions that people have experienced, have always left lasting traces on their faces throughout their lives, emphasizing more and more clearly the character and traits of each individual human.

Good characters are known after deeds...

Good characters are naturally inherited, they show respect and compassion, appreciation, consideration, love, are honest and generous, live in spirit of fighting without attacking and righteously defending themselves, receive nothing without deserving. It's easy to distinguish a good character from a bad one, due to the fact that the good one will always be there when it's hard, and the bad one will be there just when it don't have to do something for someone's benefit. Even when he gets angry, good character will overcome his anger only to lend a helping hand the one next to him, a shoulder for who is crying, and will not close the door to the distressed human if the help is asked. Here to think about the people which really are good people and have no malice in them, they don't come with hidden thoughts or have disrespect.

With the bad human have to be vigilant...

Unfortunately, opening the door for an evil human to enter your home, into your life to destroy your family and peace, it is like you were introducing the trojan horse yourself into your home. You can discover the bad people when you feel attacked by them, they only wish to harm you and cause you many problems, they even humiliate you in public, envy you for the simple fact that you exist or have something different than them. To avoid them you should know that they are very friendly, kind people, jumpy and generous beyond measure even when it is not the case, they pay attention to everything you do, only to attack you later.

Character goes hand in hand with intelligence...

Character and intelligence are person's treasures, but intelligence without character is just a waste. The intelligence of good characters is not inherited, resulting from what accumulates over the years and from the environment that surrounds them thus becoming a specific and natural characteristic.

Intelligence is a wealth, if you know how to use it...

Due to the good character, intelligence comes as a plus added to characteristic riches of educated people, who know how to achieve the purposes in their lives. They know how to behave with people around them and not to hurt anyone on their way to ascension. Never they will not touch another's property, will not to covet other people's happiness, not to envy and do not destroy others' relationships. Also, they will not harm and nor to take revenge, will not steal or lie, will avoid the temptation, the undeserved desire, the advantages by vanity and vain pride. Instead, the evil character will have the ability to advise and manipulate only in his favour.

Bad character comes only to the table seted...

The bad character will always be with you only when it needs something; when you have everything; you are happy and do not feel alone; you are happy and surrounded by the world; you are healthy and look good; when do not need anyone's help. It will know how to flatter you, it behaving accordingly to your expectations and telling you the words which you want to hear thanks to which you will allow yourself to be manipulated. After using you and taking everything it expected from you, the bad character will ignore you not caring about the consequences you will have to face. Finally, when it has drained all your energy until you have nothing left to give, it will disappear without a shred of gratitude or remorse.

The wealth does not buy the character...

There also, is much to be said about those who pretend to have a good character and deserve all respect just because they are rich, highly educated and come from traditional families. These pretensions are not at all bad even if they were motivated, because they represent nothing of value if they are not accompanied by a chosen character, wisdom and intelligence. The same with people who boast that they have the experience of life and that is enough, ignoring the intelligence and education of others whom they despise. This idea of life experience, is too pretentious and pompously imposed by some.

And as it's said, the human sanctifies the place...

Experience in life, can develop various characteristics. There are people who have experience in life because they have reached a certain age, but their lives have nothing interesting, intelligent, wise, great to take as an example or to learn something. Others may have experience in their ordinary work without much responsibility and their lives may not inspire more than of others, to be taken as models.

Valuable people distinguish themselves quickly...

Of course, there are and valuable people with life experience, which can be worthy to follow as examples. Because of their experience in a job that reflects expected success, specialized studies, a sparkling intelligence that inspires your respect, lives lived in a dignified and honest manner, all these gifts can awaken the desire to become like them. Other categories in which people are good examples, are successful people who have made a business through their work or those who have a career, artists, people of culture. All those who in addition to their natural talent, work hard to assert themselves, are good role models.

The people which do not sanctify the place...

The only category of people, who never cannot be taken as example, are politicians.

Some of them reach important positions without having the necessary and mandatory studies, the comparable skills, the required experience, which normally a citizen is obliged to prove these.

And the fact that they are appointed to positions based on politics and not competence, demonstrates their inability to be skilled, honest and impartial.

Normally, to lead a field and demonstrate the human qualities, certain knowledge, experience, studies and merits are required.

CHILDHOOD

Childhood is the period that has a different name, for each individual child. This being named according to the memories, experiences, joys and sorrows experienced in the past.

To be a child, in this so big world...

Also, childhood is the period of a child from birth to adolescence. If he is questioned about his childhood a teenager who had a happy childhood, then his answer will be positive. His childhood is the definition of innocence it was fantastic, it had education, trophies, challenges, dreams. He will describe a world like in stories with moments and many joys, wonderful memories, wonderful people who took care of his whole childhood.

Childhood is different...

But not all children had a beautiful childhood, that's why the answers differ for children who don't have very good memories or who don't want to remember that period of their childhood.

Regardless of the difficult childhood period with many shortcomings, problems and troubles, childhood is part of a person's life with ups and downs. This fact needs to be accepted by every person, in the idea of changing in the future, what was not good. The forgetting and forgiving, they make the life to be gentler and bearable. Not all people have the strength to make changes, due to the circumstances in which they lived their childhood, the years that should have kept the most beautiful memories.

Who suffers exists and who drinks of the cup of life they taste them all...

Suffering, is also, a step in the life of every human being, as is joy. As joy is desired, which brings the best gifts, it is also necessary to accept suffering which strengthens people, brings people closer to each other, or in some cases drives them away from each other.

The transition to adulthood...

The transition of children to the age of maturity, makes it possible to transform them into people positively marked by the life spent in childhood, or negatively marked by the childhood they had and the people who raised them, educated them.

That is why it is necessary for parents to watch over the child's thinking to make sure that it does not experience negative feelings, does not go through serious problems and is not attracted to certain habits which later can influence its life in a negative way.

Children were happier in the past…

A few decades ago it was difficult to be a child, as some children worked to earn their bread every day or went to school barefoot and poorly dressed. Even though life was hard, the children were happy within the family. There, in poverty they shared everything, loved each other and took care of each other, were connected spiritually and revealed their troubles to each other, helped and supported each other, they had the human connection.

In these times everything is upside down, human is driven by technology and because of this it is difficult to control a child's life. The child does not only need technology, food, expensive clothes and other things which some parents give to their children, to compensate for the lack in their lives.

The dream to be beautiful, it doesn't need shadows...

Children need the human presence, parents, grandparents, family members to interact with them. They need someone to pay attention to them, cheer them, on motivate them and control them in everything they do in their daily, occupations just like their grandparents did with their parents. Being alone and surrounded by technology, children turn into human robots who cannot relate with people, do not enjoy life and its beauties, do not know human suffering and joy, do not grow up with memories, do not have dreams and feelings.

So much technology and no humanity at all...

The children raised with technology in hand no longer have childhood; have no contact with other children and do not know how to play; do not know how to touch the plants and animals; they don't do exercise; have not memories to tell each other; they have no topics to debate, which to bring them soulful joy. For these reasons children end up being depressed; grow old in the spirit and being fed up with that life, that they haven't even lived; they are sad and without any appetite for life.

Where there is little technology, the child breathes...

In the opposite side, children with few opportunities in terms of technology, are happier than those who are given technology as a way of life. They learn to live a normal life, to get by without getting anything undeserved and when they are sad, they know how to deal with any condition, without having depression or other negative thoughts. First, they know how to ask for the help from those in their lives.

Children need very few things, to be happy. The things that they receive with great sadness, are those that come as a offering to cover the lack of parents. Often, children who feel the absence of parents in their lives, when they become adults, blame them for their absence in childhood and for all the failures which they experience throughout their lives.

CORRUPTION

Corruption is a form of bribery of entities and of people working in different fields of activity. To take what is not rightfully yours, is a great cowardice and lack of character. Corruption is the greatest plague of humanity, through which power is used to satisfy personal or group interests and which can permanently destroy the future of a country.

We raised with stories, telling the stories that we lived, and we will continue to dream stories, until the end of life...

Our great musician and composer George Enescu (1881-1955) said that: "We have lined ourselves with false models, the model of the human who succeeds easily, who manages, who knows how to make money. We have lost our morality, the manners and education. We forgot to dress nicely, to behave more elegantly. We have lost not the material bourgeoisie, but the bourgeoisie of the spirit, the spiritual nobility. We live today in a semi-cultural and upstart environment, impulsive and brutal. We are very far of what we once were..."

The fall of civilization happens only when there are in high positions people with no talent, corruptible, incompetent, without compassion, without moral values, but who have money and represent the interests of those who dictate to them.

Can corruption be stopped?

Corruption can be defeated only when the country is led by competent, honest, dignified people, who love their country, defend the interests of the citizens and the country.

Union is strength and the win is battle...

As long as anyone dares to criticize the values and history of the country without being punished, the disinterest of society is visibly demonstrated which agrees with its decay. The truth is hard to hear, but to those who hear it it is a great help.

Our great writer Ion Luca Caragiale (1852-1912) said that: "We Romanians are a world in which, if not is done or not thought too much about, we can be proud that at least is discussed very much..."

The involvement of every citizen in the fight for justice, truth and defense, leads to stopping and defeating corruption. Society can contribute to changing the future trajectory of the country, but only through involvement and action.

The corruption is a danger...

The corrupt country is without defence, without justice, development and in constant danger. When you look in the past and see what kind of humans all the peoples of the world had and then see the humans of today, you wonder what kind of people are left on the planet.

Whatever is sown will be reaped, you can't sow wheat and to reap corn...

The caricatures want to rule, and they fight among themselves for the master's whose interests they serve, showing that they are limited people, people who do not know more than is shown to them.

DESIRE

Tell me what you wish, so I can know your dreams…

Desire is a manifestation that can be considered a faceless form, dominating the feelings, turmoil, determination to act and decide. It can be likened to the constantly whispered voice which urges a human to do something, that could fulfil it. The human who wants to do something is a living human, a human who thinks and has needs that need be fulfilled. Who has no desires is like a plant in agony, because the plant cannot ask for water.

Positive desire…

Usually, the human starts with a positive desire wanting something extraordinary, to make it feel valuable, or to impress the public.

I would like to put a better flagstone on this world, that passes by without any precise direction...

Thinking about the actuality in which humanity is struggling daily crushed by the same problems, the same dreams and different ideals, we realize that through the desire for change a breath of air is taken, that is given to the dying before he dies.

Passive desire…

Desire without any purpose or action, is only a desire which does not materialize and eventually fades away, is forgotten. Only with the churning of the soul and mind which are devoid of the action of change everything is just a waste of time. Where there is recklessness and lack of interest, there can be no victory, even if there is the desire in its mental form.

Desire and contentment…

Desire and contentment, these two actions condition each other. If the desire is positive, then it can be associated with contentment. But if the desire has a negative connotation which harms a soul, then it is just a frustration that has been consumed.

DILIGENCE

The sloth runs more
And the fool walks as in cross,
But for that industrious with much work,
The time is comes and left...

How can you not be diligent, when you have the interest in receiving the reward?

Those who receive an unfair reward are the lazy ones or the corrupt, who will pay it all back in the end. Diligence is a characteristic of the wise, of the one who builds with patience and wisdom.

Building a good relationship, life passes as in heaven…

Building on a foundation of righteousness and fairness, thousands of blessings will come. No one ever lost by being industrious, it is a divine duty to earn a living. On the other hand, laziness is not a Christian attitude, which does honour to a healthy human from a physical and mental point of view. You must put the rod in the lazy human hand to catch the fish, not put the fish in his net.

How else he will value the work and effort of others?

Teach him that the salt rock must move it aside, not to sit with fear, that it will fall into his head.

Because a child comes into the world as an angel to be a joy and blessing to his parents. But those who leave the child into his will to be a lazy, careless, without a sense of duty, without respect and mercy, without love and consideration; then those parents grow a wild tree, which in the end will not bear any good fruit.

Diligence should be in the place of honour with wisdom, otherwise the house will fall over the human, and he will not know that it needs to save itself, will lie in the bed as lazy he's, waiting for others to do something for him.

EQUALITY

For some time, it has been repeated everywhere that people are equal and that they have equal rights. But this idea comes to disorient people, denying them the state in which they really are, making them believe that they are something else or someone else, with the purpose of being manipulated in the promises of politicians.

I don't see myself, being like you,
For my mother is not and yours,
My father doesn't belong to you either,
Why do you invoke equality?

Are people treated the same everywhere, so that they can be said to be equal?

Is the door opened to a poor human in a luxury hotel, in the same way that it is opened for a rich human?

Does a poor human can afford to eat, in the same restaurant as the rich human?

Then, where is the equality between people and how is the image of human reflected in the eyes of another human?

Of course, here it also depends on the strength of character of each human. The idea that we are all equal would be good and true, only if we refer to the fact that we all come into the world in the same way and that we all leave the world in the same way, no one is immortal.

Equality is used as a manipulation…

Otherwise, everything is a manufactured lie, which politicians trumpet with the aim of fulfilling political interests; to manipulate the public; to make the people hate each other, by putting the lie on an equal footing with the truth; unfairness on an equal footing with the fairness; the abnormal above the normal; destroying the values and promoting the grotesque; imposing everything that is worthless, with the intention of destroying everything that represents value and quality; all this for the purpose of holding power and total control of mankind.

The words equality, brotherhood and justice, sound nice, but they are good for manipulation...

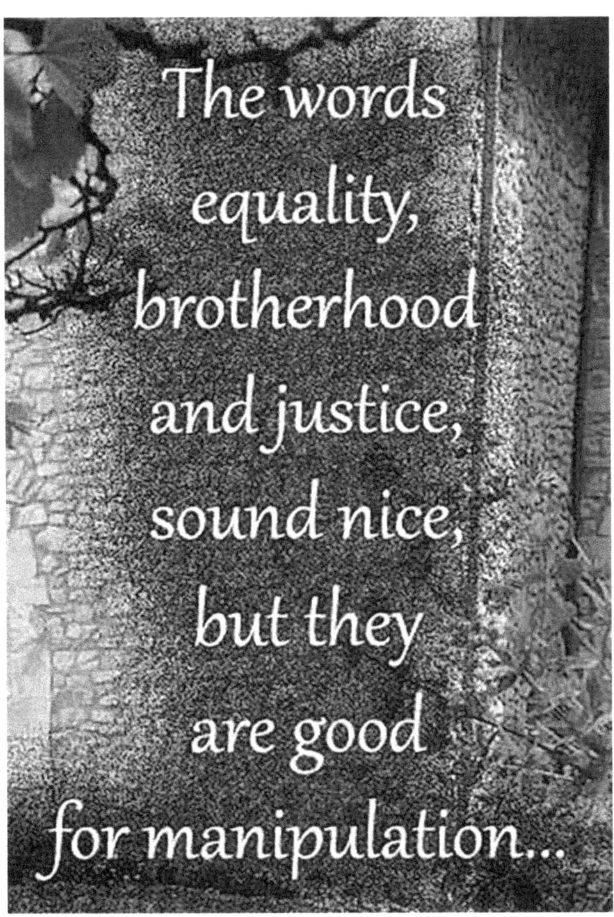

Human character is shaped…

Human inherits character, which is shaped throughout life depending on education which he receives, of the studies which he has, the way he perceives and lives his life according to skills which he owns in relation to others, by the faith and the personal convictions.

People are different…

All these factors differentiate us as people, as characters throughout our lives and make us to see more clearly the fact that not all people are the same. And as such, there are certain rules to be followed of common sense, that should be developed better, to bring us down to earth in the logical thinking and in visible practice.

The invocation of equality destroyed man…

Consequently, from this point of invoking equality the fall of human began, forming the behaviours that do not match human values, forcing people to accept the abnormal as normal.

People differ more by their actions, than by the words they say…

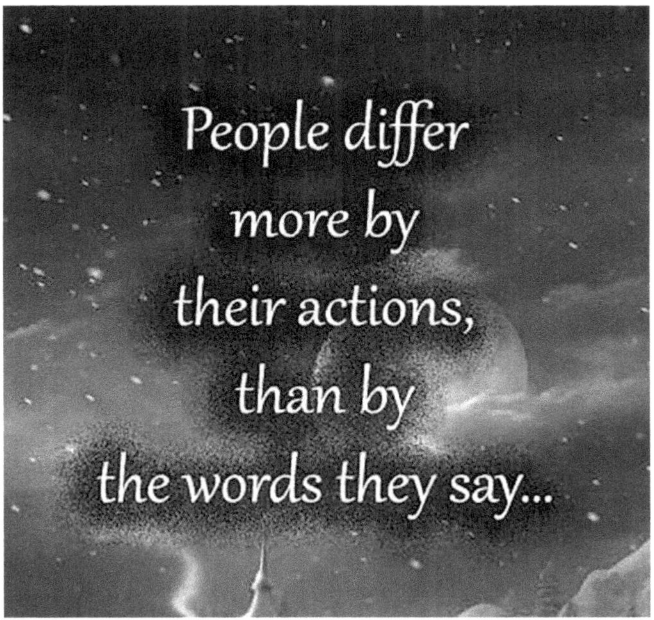

They always say something and something else is out…

For these reasons, people have transformed and continue to transform into beings difficult to recognize and imagine. Some want to be something else than as nature gave them and others have isolated themselves from people, living like savages after so many centuries of human emancipation, wanting more and more the disappearance of civilization.

In addition, other categories of people were developed for example the liars, the corrupt people, criminals, thieves, misers, the wicked and inhumane, the depraved and unscrupulous, all have multiplied worse than everything and they are destroying the world.

Then how are we all equal, if we are not the same and do not act according to the same principles and rules?

Who is right in the end?

Those who hold the power because they distribute the justice, that justice which is seen and perceived by their eyes full of bizarre and inhuman interests?

And some people still dreaming, saying that we are all equal in this world.

But let's not get drunk with cold water…

FEAR

Fear is a disturbing sensation, which causes human to make hasty decisions. This state primarily includes human who does not have a relationship with God and being at the mercy of the chance in this world.

When you don't have a pole of which to lean on, you fall...

I'm afraid to dream,
When the wind whistles in ruins,
Then I wake up in a hurry,
From dream, where you were with me...

Fearful people will always do reckless things, make bad decisions under pressure and end up living like as the guinea pigs locked in a cage, at the discretion of whoever tests them through various fear-induced states.

Fear prevents thinking...

Fear is the hindrance to discerning the situation and making well-thought-out decisions. It is like placing a veil over the eyes to see nothing in that moment of fear, loss of thought and calm.

Fear makes man sick...

On the other hand, premeditated fear sickens the soul and mind of the tormented, keeping him captive in imagined thoughts and turmoil. And weak people, without confidence and strength in them, are the most suitable victims of fear.

Fear not, little flock... it says in the bible...

Encouragement easily crosses the threshold of fear which gives courage in decision-making, helps to keeping hope, to build and complete any project that seems impossible at first.

I can, because I can,
Divinity tells me,
That I'm strong and that's all...

The brave human cannot be enslaved, by any human weakness. It will always preserve its dignity, integrity and rights due to it.

The fearful human is lacking in action...

Just like that and the fearful person sits quietly in her portion of space without daring more, without hoping more, without acting more for various reasons and excuses. While the brave person gets involved with great momentum in any field, risking everything without fear.

Politicians are the best examples of weeds growing everywhere, occupying everything, owning and mastering everything, while capable and competent people stand aside because of the fear of failure.

Therefore, there are two categories of people, those without courage who have frustrations and brave people who play their last card, regardless of what comes next.

For this reason, the latter end up being the former and the former end up being led by people who are not always honest.

Usually, this world is ruled by the corrupt materialists, opportunists and those without a bit of human conscience.

FORGIVENESS

To forgive it is a big thing,
When the enemy hit,
But to know it doesn't hurt,
When you stay away from a mad...

Forgiveness is the light of love...

By loving people, you give them the forgiveness because love opens the door of the heart, and forgiveness is given to everyone with a wide hand, because the divinity made us to be good and forgivers.

But forgiveness is never a good sister to stupidity...

The forgiven must learn something, from the chance given to him by the wronged one. If it is unable to change, then it is not entitled for any more forgiveness, because it has a corruptible and weak character. Will always lie and manipulate the person, who gave it a chance. Forgive, but don't forget that you forgave, because that's the only way you'll know how to protect yourself.

Forgiveness is only for people who have made mistakes, but strive to change through the positive actions and attitudes.

The Bible says not to give pearls to swine...

I mean, don't let anyone fool you, and when you're fooled, take a stand to remember so it doesn't happen again.

FRIENDSHIP

Guard your heart, so as not to enters whoever in it...

The friendship, this word so sweet, but which sometimes leaves a very bitter taste, it is based on fairness, respect, honesty, dedication, esteem, purity of soul, joy for friends, mutual and altruistic help, on the qualities normally associated with the common sense.

Friendship versus love...

The friendship based on the soulful feelings, should not be confused with love based on the physical, carnal attraction. When they are young and without family obligations women and men have a special friendship and from friends they can turn into lovers or husbands. But in the case of a family, it is normal for spouses to introduce their life partner to friends, forming new friendships that can last a lifetime. From the moment a person starts a family, it is necessary to be devoted to the family, spend time with the person it loves and give it all the attention deserves. In a united family, spouses take care of each other, so that they do not suffer for any reason which could intervene, because of friends or other people.

It is not good that one spouse stays at home, while the other spouse meets its friends to party, this may destroy the married person's relationship.

Of their kind, and by human nature, people are selfish and defends its own interests...

Some people, usually those who have a hidden and unstable character, overcome the barriers of friendship by maintaining a hidden relationship with partners in their circle. Thus, causing irreparable suffering in the lives of their partners, even ending up living by the advice suggested by their friends. In this case it can no longer be about friendship, but only about the interest in getting something, the destruction of the friend's relationship with the partnerner, physical or sentimental attraction, attention, admiration or even some benefits at the expense of someone else.

Friendship out of interest...

In these times, most friends are looked for only when some needed, most of the time they are used and then abandoned. So, some people who have not spoken for a long time, suddenly they remember the existence of an old friendship to get a favour, a common interest, or simply based on a necessary funding.

The interest wears the hat…

If that friendship is based only on interest, then it will end the moment there is no reason for collaboration or the need to use of each other.

The friendship from the past...

Friendship of the time of our grandparents and parents was based on comradeship, respect, consideration, chosen friendship, mutual help, unconditional love, living together when needed, shared joys resulting from the victories of a friend's success, common interests without selfishness.

The friends that appear like shadows, without bringing any sun, you don't have to come ahead to them...

There are some people who accept to be used by friends in their circle, just out of a desire not to be alone. They associate with people who lack character and consideration, who don't care who they use, their goal being to fulfill their own well-defined needs and desires.

The strong man, nor the rain does moves him and neither does the storm...

In general, the man who inherits a strong character, will seek not to answer the call of those who have used it and caused it some damage or inconvenience by manipulating him to his disadvantage. Because it knows that who used it once, doesn't deserve to be given another chance to use it. And anyone who says that he is wrong, doesn't deserve to be given, too much chances.

Otherwise, it will think that it is its duty to err and everyone else to accept him as is, as some say as an excuse. It is certain that no human deserves a chance, without proving by good deeds that it has a beautiful character.

Why to accept a person with good and bad?

The human should to work on its character and learn not to make mistakes, grow in knowledge and in respect, to get closer to the person which he has harmed, even more so when meets a quality person.

Open your heart to the one who seeks you today, for the time will come when no one look for you...

We know that friendship is a relationship above everything and within friendship all thoughts, dreams, regrets, revelations are consumed. Who comes into possession of these values, owns the spiritual wealth of the one who revealed them to it. That's why, a friend knowing you is the first person in the world to protect your back, so that no one does you any harm. It is the first to put you on guard, when you are on the wrong path. It is the first to rejoice of your accomplishments and defends you from all evils.

Not all who say they are friends, are friends...

Who attacks the goods, joys, relationships, every-thing that belongs to its friend, is an envious sinner who stood always been in the shadow of his friend. Being satisfied, just with the remains that could be collected from its friend's life, which it envied it and betrayed him behind or in front, as often as it had occasion. Such people are the ones without character, who don't deserve to be a part of anyone's life, and everyone should put them aside without regrets.

GREED

The glutton is on,
Gathering and gathering,
In the end it is taking nothing,
When it descends into the grave...

Greed is a disease of fools, of those who can't get enough to collecting and they can't sleep peacefully, because of their fortunes. God gave everything that exists on the earth for all people without distinction, the only difference would be, that everyone should work for what they want to have. It is not fair for a lazy human to impose, to have everything the same as the industrious has, but neither the thief should not steal from where he didn't put anything. The world is full of such people, who amass riches to boast, to rule, to corrupt, and to carry out their deceptive plans. It is the same when someone takes money from the poor, is certainly robbing them, and whoever takes money from the rich is declared their slave. The human who collects without stopping, at a given moment it becomes ill from the worries of wealth and all wealth is of no use to it anymore.

HAPPINESS

We are fleeting lights...

Happiness can't be bought or sold, it's like the moon in the sky that you admire, but you can't touch it when you want. Anyone who says that being happy is easy, is just saying that they are wrong.

Happiness is not a mask...

Also, happiness is not a mask under which someone hides, pretending and showing the smile of happiness, which is just a lie with a shield, because happiness is not the same as blindness. And to taste happiness, you don't need to buy happiness by bribing the people or running after every temptation that comes in your way.

Happiness is the simplest equation...

Human soul should always be happy, in this equation lies the recipe for happiness. The wise human is happy in the state in which he is, with whom is and where is because he builds, he does not waste time endlessly dreaming up various scenarios of happiness. Human builds happiness seriously and naturally using the human values, laying healthy foundations, that do not harm those around whom it builds its happiness. Happiness means do not carry a task behind you that you could not complete this, or you can do wrong. That is to be the aware, constantly, about your possibilities that you really have, the physically and the mentally.

Nobody is happy, forever…

There are times when happiness is replaced with the unhappiness. But this should not change us in any way, we should accept our situation by looking for a correct remedy and that will not harm other couples. The problem of unhappiness came in when we built a relationship with who was not supposed to, it was certain interests, or we were simply deceived into believing too much in that person, who only wanted a relationship for the moment.

Not all people are equally skilled in relationships…

Happy relationships are formed out of the people who meet in their youth and really love each other, they have the same dreams, projects, pleasures, ideals, they are compatible in everything, and they create a relationship from scratch.

A relationship made up of pieces, is not like a whole one…

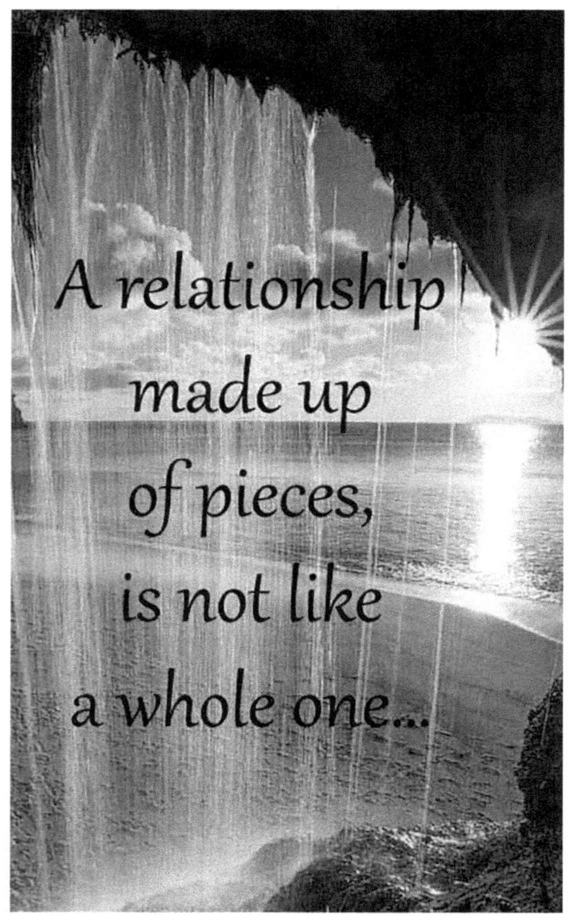

The rest of the relationships are very rare which can be happy, because there is no longer a single relationship between a man and a woman, there are relationships, families and children in some couples. And when a couple is formed from people who have had other relationships, marriages, that couple comes with the baggage of every earlier relationship. For these reasons, you can consider yourself the lucky human who met a good person, or you can be in a torturous situation for the whole time you stay in that relationship. It's all like a lottery, but every human assumes their own risk, knowing all these things beforehand.

It's not normal to destroy the peace of human…

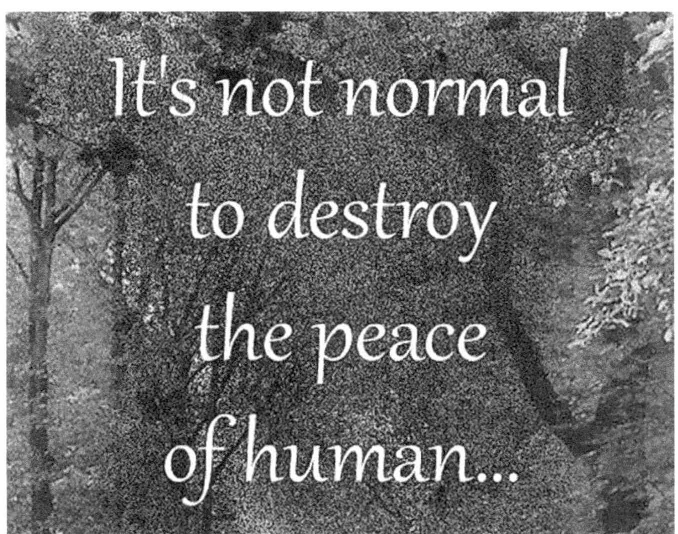

Therefore, it is no one's fault, and no one should ruin another's life. Normally, educated people, intelligent and sensible they break up on amicable terms and each human goes his own way. It's not easy to break up a relationship, but it's healthier for unhappy people do not be together and not make their lives difficult. The worst part is that some people stay in relationships and betray their partners, thinking that they will be happy, and in the end, they turn out to be characterless people who do more harm than good.

Why don't people get along?

People connect with all kinds of environments where they meet different people and these people in turn can bring happiness or unhappiness in one's life. It always depends on the bonds that are strengthened and the purpose of continuing the relationship with the people you meet by chance or for life.

Relationships that are not forced, are the successful ones…

The relationships between the people who have natural, disinterested, common connections and from the same backgrounds, bond more closely and can last longer. While relationships that are sustained only for some interest or purpose, they grow cold after being consumed and do not always have a happy ending. When a door closes, a gate can be opened after it. Just need courage, strength, determination and never to looking back.

In the past, people married those of their rank…

In the time of our grandparents and parents, relations between people were much closer, because people kept their relations with those of their own condition and did not interfere with each other. There were certain barriers which were not allowed to be crossed, but people were happier, even if they were limited.

HELPLESSNESS

I would like to do the good,
But my precarious condition,
It makes me small and too poor,
To can afford a burden...

Sometimes we want to do the great things, but that desire is hindered somewhere by a lack of energy, potential or even will. Then we stop in the middle, not being able to continue at least one more step. That happens when the human gets stuck, it has neither the strength and nor the solution to figure out the completion, because the success does not always depend on the one who wants to fight and believes in success.

What should you do?

When one feels that he is stuck somewhere, it should seek the solution in silence and peace, because silence speaks best. And who believes in God, should close its eyes and to pray. To admit that he cannot move forward, to ask to be strong and to know that needs help. Because anyone who asks for something with the confidence that it will be received, should be answered, because that is the law of nature. It is given to you after the strong faith you should have, that you will receive what you ask. In this case we are referring to the positive things, because you will not receive anything from God, if you ask to harm someone in your favour.

Ask and it shall be given to you...knock and it shall be opened to you...

In the end, that man to think logically about the problem that is bothering him and when it doesn't work, this can mean that need to find another solution, or it should be given up.

If it is a couple relationship?

If a relationship doesn't work, it needs to stop in time without continuing the ordeal of pain, reproaches, blows and destruction, which in the end will triumph regardless of the other's desire. Cannot build a structure too great for your strength, even if a man can move mountains from their place, other can't moving a human without his will to action.

Be dignified, open, courageous and say stop...

In this way will be save two people, who are not suitable to walk the same road. And when the relationships with other are harmful, can give them up, because no one is forced to sit next to bad humans.

INFIDELITY

Only the fool who doesn't know,
That betrayal will be paid,
Stealling all on the debt,
More and more is losing...

Ivan Turgeniev (1818-1883) said that "man's most unfaithful mistress is hope: it deceives him daily, but he lives with it all his life..."

Sometimes you don't have to put soul where there is no soul, because not everyone deserves you. Give what you get; if you get love, then give love; if you receive attention, then give attention; if someone respects you, then do the same; if you get trouble, then defend yourself; if you don't get love, then do not give the pearls to swine.

People make mistakes...

The people who miscalculate lives, marry inappropriate people, and later they want the freedom to live in the way they want, but without considering the presence of the partners that they have attracted into their relationships. Such people turn out to be immature and indecisive, liars in promises, without character, without dignity and respect, without wisdom, thieves of feelings who can betray their completely innocent partners, destroying their lives.

They are not responsible...

Because they don't take responsibility to leaving a relationship not being able to continue it and even though they stay in that relationship, they make a lot of mess around themselves and of others. So that, in addition to lives of partners, they also destroy other lives that depend on the relationship with them. And all just for the pleasure of cheating, that they to feels wanted and by others from outside of marriage. Lost people, with unimaginable selfishness and dangerous at the same time. By the recklessness to marry not recognizing that a marriage or a relationship with them brings suffering, trouble and pain, they enter in false relationships and weave ruined lives around them. When you like to fly like a leaf in the wind, it is better to be alone, because it is the healthiest for anyone around you.

Infidelity is known to be punishable by law…

And if someone dares to destroy the lives around, then it will receive from life what it gave, because no deed goes unpunished.

Such relationships where there is betrayal or reasons by which it appears that a partner is unfaithful, should be ended at once. That unfaithful human will never stop betraying the relationship, regardless with who it is, will keep looking. The problem is that such people false in terms of relationships and stability meet wonderful people in their lives, whom they trick into attracting them, then torture them with their betrayals.

They enjoy torturing others...

For these people, it is a pleasure to torture someone. Also, are very different from those they attract, have nothing in common being very limited, without a baggage of knowledge or intelligence, they are not open to discussion or anything that might make them seem special. Even more so is the fact that, they cheat on their partners with people of their level, far below the level and quality of the partners which they are cheating on. It is precisely, here is the most painful thing for the deceived, to see that they are replaced with caricatures people who are very inferior to them. This is the idea that these deceivers convey, that everyone is much better, apart from their life partners with they live with. Their only skills are to lure people and manipulate them, to lie and cheat them without any shame, only to then get bored of the current victims and to look for new ones. They are like vampires who use people's energy, easily turning them from normal people into hypnotized, people who after they recover, can't believe that they were involved in such a story. No one should play with someone else's life, by destroying it just because they wanted a momentary toy, that they got bored of and wanted to throw away. In this world everything returns both good and bad, because beyond this world human walks with nothing.

Life is too short anyway, why should you shorten it yourself?

They are wise people who understand that being unfaithful in a relationship, is not a Christian or human habit. But there are also these perverts, who never deserve to be in a relationship. There would be a lot to say in these situations where cheated people get into relationships, where they have no reason to be in but as they say, every human has a reason to be there. Everything stays up to the victim to decide, what to do in such situations. The best solution would be for everyone to go their separate ways, for that abuser to receive his legal punishment, in the case of divorce and in other cases it will be a trauma and a life lesson.

KINDNESS

Forget me that I still exist,
Even though you were in my life,
I withdraw because I can't resist,
I can no longer bear your presence...

Humanity is derived from the word man, meaning the supreme being who has strength, character, will, love and consideration for his fellowmen.

Aristotle (384 BC-322 BC) said that "The wise man does not say what it thinks, but what it says, it thinks..."

When you pronounce the word human, you mean the fruitful collaborative relationships between people, the help given when needed, charitable deeds, chosen behaviours, deeds of humanity. But, in addition to all these beautiful words, attributed to humanity there is also the word inhuman which derives from man without humanity without feelings and without proper behaviour. Mans without humanity, should be avoided by everyone, like weeds from flowers. We live in a world, where many do not know what humanity means. Humanity means the normality; the normal people who have a family and children; assume their married life in holy purity, without their minds to wandering towards the sin.

These people believe in God and enjoy the life, as their parents were with temperance and wisdom. They stretch themselves as much as they can and do not covet what does not belong to them. They do good, as much as their material condition allows them. They do not like to come into conflict with others or cause scandals. Are full of humanity, wisdom and intelligence, people pleasing to God. The virtues of these people consist primarily of fairness and common sense, normality, truth and goodness, the humanity that makes them better and different from the rest of the world.

LIE

The lie with short legs,
Whoever seeks it to know,
That it has nowhere to hide,
Of the truth which will come...

A small lie is as big as a huge lie, a lie is a lie, and it gets bigger when it is hidden. It starts from a defensive reason, in which a person tries to excuse a certain behaviour or an action. The problem is that some lies lead to disasters, destroying the lives and futures of those involved in the scenario of the lie. It cannot be said that there are saviour lies, because person burdens itself soulfully with every lie assuming the consequences and because every lie, brings a loss to someone. The human accustomed to lying, will never be able to do good to anyone, being accustomed to living selfish and disregarding any human it is lying to. That human betrays and deceives without blinking, looking you in the eye and lying with nonchalance and impudence. These specimens are very harmful, even is worse, if they are among those of the same blood, or in a marriage relationship. The solution to any lie would be that when it occurs it should be solved on the spot, in this way the problems will decrease, and the losses will be much smaller. It is not good to argue with the lying man, because puts you to shame in public and becomes very aggressive in privacy. So, to run away from the crafty human lest he draw you into his side and to become like him, for the devil is also crafty, and that human serves him.

LOVE

The Holy Apostle Paul: 3-67, says in the Christian Bible that "Love is long-suffering, love is benevolent, love does not hate, doesn't brag, is not proud. Love does not behave improperly, does not look for her own, does not get angry, does not think evil. Does not rejoice in injustice but rejoices in the truth. Suffers all, believes all, hopes all, endures all. Love never fails..."

This is how we can define love in whatever generation we live in, because people need remain people.

Love resists until betrayal...

Love endures everything until it is betrayed, because betrayal is not equal to love, them are totally different and who loves never betrays.

Mistake should be proven…

Love is lenient with people who do wrong without realizing it and who are sorry for what they have done to the detriment of others, striving to right the wrong.

Love has qualities...

Love does not make enemies, because it has no reason to be negatively charged, it is justice and truth, light and love. Love does not boast of what is not its due unjustly and without work. Love does not boast with praises and vain actions, just for the sake of ggrandizement, but demonstrates through real facts. Who has love does not misbehave with others does not seek his advantages at the expense of others does not get angry needlessly does not think of harming anyone, doesn't make mistakes on purpose to mislead.The man possessed by love, does not rejoice when there is injustice and always fights for the truth. Love believes everything until the moment the truth is known and then she becomes categorical.

No one should play with the love...

Love is not lost, except when someone hurts a person causing it to walk away hurt and disappointed.

The agape love...

This agape love is the best feeling of the human soul as the Bible describes it. This is love we have for God, our involvement in helping people through charity and good deeds. It is love that lays aside all other shortcomings, accepting them in their natural state and giving of itself totally without expectation.

Love is not empty words...

Love is not just words spoken without deeds to impress, attract and sway people's minds. That's why regardless of the place where there is love, there is also God, the good deeds and people who fight for peace, justice and truth. The mouth that utters the word love, is sealed with the seal of normality, truth, peace and good understanding between all the people of the planet.

Love is the freedom…

Love means the freedom in the spirit of justice, not the freedom of abnormality, that misleads the acceptance imposed on others in the idea of saying that it is obligatory, to love what is actually contradictory to what we detest.

Love is love, meaning light and acceptance...

To close your eyes and say only with your mouth that there is love, when in fact there is imposition, means to strip ourselves of our dignity as people who can make the distinction between good and bad, ugly and beautiful, grotesque and extraordinary.

MANHOOD

The definition of masculinity is shaped by a man's character and intelligence, when he faces the challenges of making mature decisions, so as to demonstrate a man's strength of character at all stages of life.

A wise man, is who puts his love in Creator who gave him a name…

Generally, the wise man is not concerned with the muscles formed by the physical exertion, but he is unceasingly concerned with the enrichment of the virtues inherited and learned throughout his life.

What should a man's character to include of?

The most important of all virtues is the patience. With the patience, a man goes through circumstances and temptations, can make decisions appropriate to the situation, does not lose its temper by getting angry, does not lose itself in vain thoughts when it is sad, builds and maintains a lasting and stable relationship.

I think of you rare flower,
Which God has given to me,
With a beautiful spring smell,
In which you lured me...

In addition to the patience that fulfills them all, the thinking of the man about decisions taken, the quality of his soul, the way he treats his own freedom and the freedom of others, the behavior in society and in the family also matter.

With my hand I can lift,
Your little worries,
To wipe your sweat a little,
Which is drain over your forehead...

The virtues of manhood which reveals the strength of a man, are reflected in the actions taken by the man in the face of real life problems, the way he responds to the hard blows, injustices and challenges for which he has to fight hard. Women are interested in admiring at a man character, stability, honesty, honor, intelligence, wisdom, dignity, purity of soul, spirit of justice, fight for the truth.

I think about you every night,
Beautiful flower of my soul,
You know I send you love in whispers
And I always hold you to my chest...

Caring for the woman create the feeling of safety and the certainty that she is loved, the man causes her to consider him worthy of respect, to show him admiration and love, always feeling safe with him.

Handsome at the body, ugly to the soul...

The beautiful character is the beauty of the man, which he discovers it to the woman when he establishes a relationship with her and no other woman has a place in the mind of the wise man who gives himself to only one woman.

Ugly manhood...

The ugliness of manhood is the failures of man who goes through life without having learned anything, the lack of any courage, the cowardly flight from all difficulties and problems that should strengthen him and solve them, the lack of compassion and love, the lack of honesty and dialogue, betrayal of relationship, noninvolvement in the relationship, the lying, the instability, delusion, hidden nature, vain talking, impatience, misunderstanding, neglect, selfishness, laziness, avarice.

The man who is not honest, he does not love justice

He who does not know what love is, does not accept stability either. He does not take care of the purity of his soul, not persist in good things, does not like forgiveness, not believe in self-sacrifice, cannot form a chosen soul, is not good and honest, is always driven by hidden vices and the passions of moment.

Man should not forget that he is born of a woman, raised and educated by a woman, loved and admired by a woman. And if the woman does not have the stable balance next to a man, then that man does not deserve her. As the man is called the priest of the house, before whom the woman comes to talk about her joys, sorrows, plans and her most secret thoughts, the man should listen to her with patience and love, advise her wisely, support her in the fulfillment of her plans good and fairs.

I come to you my love,
My pains to cry,
To put my thoughts in his hands,
To the only man on the earth.

All the duties of the man, once they are fulfilled, they adjust to the power of manhood.

We are lights that extinguish......

The beauty and strength of the man's body will pass, but the woman who is his fulfilment as a capable and responsible man, will remain by his side until the end of their lives. If the man was like a good priest, lovingly and patiently advised the woman who brought him all the joys of the world, then he will enjoy love and respect in a quiet life.

Each human how will make the bed, this is how it will sleep...

Our grandparents used to say that every human chooses to live its life, as it pleases. Manhood is the part of wisdom and responsibility of the man who in case of a failure in a relationship he does not blame anyone, but assumes his mistakes, by working on his character and behavior, so as not to repeat the mistakes made.

Silence is an emerald,
Which sanded is made,
In an unforgettable love,
When hearts unite to make peace.

Instead the defeated and unwise man discovers his helplessness and weak character, proving that he was not worthy of the role at the head of his family, disappointing them through the decisions made. He did not know how to treat the family and was not patient enough, indulgent, constant in love, showed no interest or even appreciation for the woman he claimed to love. He did not fulfill his duties as a man, was not fair and honest causing the woman to act in the same way.

It's your fault you did not know,
When tears was flow strings,
When the soul in sadness stayed silent,
And you were watching how I cry and how it hurts...

And if the woman lost her value, then it was the man who produced this thing, by the way he treated the woman to whom he swore his love when they stepped into a new life. If the man's words and deeds were valid for the moment, then he received what he gave, a momentary love and listening.

Man is woman's mirror...

The wise, honest, intelligent and well-intentioned man is the one who does not change his behaviour and interest towards the woman he loves, because he knows that the woman gives back everything she receives.

What expectations does the man have who is not a follower of what he wanted and promised, not being constrained by anyone?

The problem is that...

Why does a man fall in love with a woman for whom he would give everything in the beginning and then he pay no attention to it, having the pretension for the woman to remain as he knew her, loving, attentive and faithful as at the beginning?

Why they can?

There are some men who live even over a hundred years with the same women and who say that if they had to start over they would do the same.

The secret of coexistence...

It is definitely the fact that they keep their promises to the women in their lives and do not give them the opportunity to act otherwise than in the right and honest way.

Emancipation misunderstood…

False emancipation has contributed much to the destruction of the family and manhood, the excessive display of pornography has stolen the minds of some causing them to see opportunities, that have led them to give up their life partners because of monotony and boredom. Men were the ones who started the destruction of relationships.They began by flirting anywhere and with anyone, hiding their double lives from their wives. At the same time, building other relationships with women without conscience and common sense, destroying everything they once built with love.

Suddenly, your feet was on fire,
After the woman who once see you,
You began to see her even in dreams,
Weak man, you lost your mind...

Disintegration has destroyed families...

Some, even when they were with their life partners, did not hold back to break their hearts and turning them into frustrated, angry, vengeful, betrayed and destroyed women. Having enough reason, wives began to deprive their husbands of due respect considering them heartless traitors, who deserved their hatred and contempt.

You looked at another enchanted,
Believing the world belongs to you,
And you seem have forgotten me,
You didn't know I was with you...

The disappointment was more accentuated when the wives saw how their husbands break their word very easily at the appearance of other women, who were looking for victims. Thus, masculinity was destroyed entitling women to believe that it is difficult or even impossible, to trust a man without suspicion him. From these behaviours three categories of people with effects on masculinity resulted. The first category is the hunting men and the women who allow themselves to be hunted, being available at any time for certain favours, interests or money.

Do you like hunting,
To leave proud and tidy,
Carefully smoothing your path,
The deceiver who lied to me.

Family values...

The second category is the one that believes in family values although is attacked by the environment in which it lives and is always forced to transform and live as the rest of the world lives. People who really want a family and not for some reason, have the highest sense of duty. They are honest, open and transparent in everything they do, they really love each other by taking care of each other, are patient, understand each other in all things, help each other, are constant in their feelings and attitudes, are forgiving and good listeners, they have compassion, consideration and respect.

Family is a wealth,
Which in the world God left,
That spouses, always support to be,
When the one falls and it's hard for it.

The third category which is the destruction of masculinity, are men who no longer want to be men. Although they have male bodies, they like to imitate women in everything they do in their daily lives, imitating them by their behaviors and clothing, also pretending to be women.

You turned into a woman,
Wanting a life like mine,
You walk around in a lady's dress,
But you also you know don't have something.

MISER

The miser who runs a lot,
to collect the money,
does not enjoy,
he don't share the wealth,
which slave keeps him...

Avarice is a disease that sickens the fragile person from the mental point of view, by injecting its eyes with the image of money which it constantly counts. So the miser's only happiness is to count his money often, to know that he has it in a safe place.

The well from which no water is drunk, eventually turns into an fountain with undrinkable water...

Avarice can not only be considered a material evil for the human structure, but it can also exist as a sentimental evil, in which people want to receive the multitude of feelings which they are not able to return.

I give you my love now,
Without to know you give something return,
With you I want to count immortality,
With you to leave this earth...

Instead generosity is like a spring that flows continuously, bringing fresh water. The more you give, the more the pathways open for abundance and blessing to flow.

Who gives a penny,
To that one, who stretches the hand,
To himself gives, does not waste,
It makes the world more beautiful...

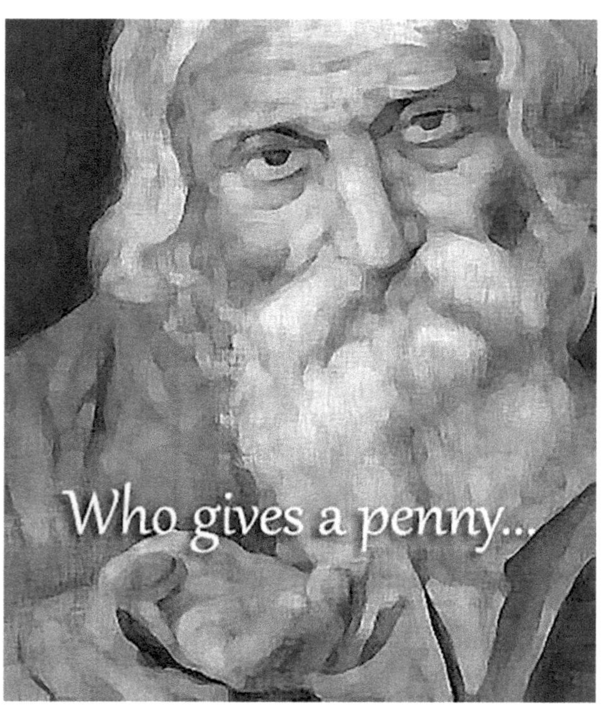

MONEY

Of whom the human idolizes, that will be his master...

Fraudulently obtained money influences the weak characters bringing them into the state of lawlessness, abuse of power, corruption, injustice, buying and selling all what they want.

Nothing is forbidden to money,
Nothing stands before them and is not holy,
Money is man's punishment,
Which takes it to the grave with him...

Because of the power obtained through the possession of money, corrupt people become idols. These idols are worshiped by those who serve them and fulfill their commands, being loyal to them. The money invested for the development of society and all of humanity, represents the currency of exchange in the development process, but money remains money.

I gave you money
And you should remember,
That it is a duty to be loyal,
To who hands you the money...

You will answer me for the money,
Which in your hand take shelter,
You will make bargain and with the enemies,
That I don't throw money, I don't spend it...

RESPONSIBILITY

I did it
And now forgive me,
That I broke your heart into pieces,
But we each have a fate...

Someone's responsibility is not a word spoken in the wind...

Only the misleading minds towards their calculated targets, they can play with the responsibility of decisions, actions and facts. Any responsibility brings a loss to someone, having decisive consequences for the future and the course of life. When you bring a child into the world, it is a great responsibility about its education and future, can't being able to say that just being born is enough. And the moment of the decision to unite your life with someone, this is still a very big responsibility. Human, who comes into your life has the certainty that you know what you are doing, that you will be its half, everything will be finally a whole, you will be its heart, eyes, mind and right hand. But you play saying that's how it was meant to be and other nonsense, when you harm that person. It wasn't meant to be, only your prickly nature wanted to pierce someone's life and cause blood to flow.

Never play with human loyalty, because eventually it will get tired of your teasing and walk out of your life forever. The loyal person who is with you at good and bad, encourages and supports you, it is a treasure. Loyalty also has its limits, but if you go beyond the limits and cause the respective person to move away from you, through the disappointments you cause, through the behaviours with which you upset or humiliate it because of others, then the day will come when it will tell you that it is got fed up. And when he gets fed up, it will change everything, giving you back what you gave to it.

Also, the leadership of a country entails the most colossal responsibility, for all citizens of that nation.

Historian Nicolae Iorga (1871 – 1940) said that "A people that does not know its history, is like a child that does not know its parents."

The correctness of those who lead a country it is decisive and capital, giving birth to people who will lead or to be monsters oppress.

Historian Nicolae Iorga (1871 – 1940) also said that "The vices are the executioners that kill you slowly, like an unsharpened sword."

RICHES

The most precious wealth of person is faith, because without believing in something you have no strength to move on to get up from your knees and fight.

Human without God is the poorest human…

Who has any faith,
Its heart will be rich,
When will be it in distress,
It has a door to knock on...

Love of people is a continual disappointment, but love of God is a promise. When you get close to God you no longer need anything, because he is everything and you are no longer a lonely person. Health is a precious gift received at man's birth, but which man does not value until he lose her.

Family is the person next to you...

Family is the most precious gift that people enjoys. The family is the mother, the one who in addition to her great suffering to give you life, she sees you even at 100 years old her helpless child, the one to whom she gives everything she has until the last her breath. The family is the father, the one who works for his children, to have all the necessities of life often making sacrifices beyond his human powers. The family is the child who understands the great sacrifice made by those who brought him into the world to raise him; giving him from their youth, their work and their bread from the mouth; their sleepless nights and making it possible to fulfill children dreams. Family is any person who lives with you, eats with you, sleeps with you under the same roof, loves and values you, is the support and fulfillment through which you know that your life has a meaning.

The family also has responsibilities...

The family has the duties of respect, honesty, understanding, consideration, suffering, comradeship, stability, trust, transparency, giving, noble love, compassion, care, acceptance, sacrifice, truth, support, patience, admiration, forgiveness.

The good people who encourage you to get up and they follow your every step with joy, those are a real blessing. The inherited language, the way of life and the traditions of the nation, all these are immeasurable riches of a self-respecting people and have right to exist, to continue.

Our language is a treasure,
From the depths it rises,
To say that in the past,
She was carved into the rock...

The riches of the country...

All the hills, the waters, the lands, the plains, the mountains over which animals and the birds fly freely, all these are the riches of the country for which the people must fight and to preserve them as they inherited them from their ancestors, with the dream to have an inheritance the descendants. If all these inherited gifts are not kept in their place of honor, then that people is deprived of its national identity and is condemned to extinction.

Over the ancestral tongue,
Let there be no other language,
That our country is Romanian,
We didn't come here from wandering...

There was once a world where people had little, or no schooling, but who had a lot of humanity, Romanian identity, dignity and respect for God.

Our country bears gold,
Over the woven robes,
Of skilful hands which once,
They could to move even a mountain...

Who does not love his country,
He has no family and no estate,
It's small the world for him
And he stay away wandering.

He has nowhere, to go
And nowhere he to turn,
No one is waiting for him at home,
To hug him in the gate...

ROMANTIC LOVE

For poets, romantic love represents the chosen feelings, which all together make up a noble love, given with reverence to the adored person. The poet sings the love, romance, carnal and soul attraction, gathering them all in a bundle, which he places at the feet of beloved woman. Love belongs to the feelings of women, inspiring songs and poems, the adoration of melancholic and pleasant dance.

Love without soul love, is nothing...

It can be sensual and cruel, bringing with it unrequited pleasure and pain, carried deep into the lives of captive souls who cannot detach themselves from their state of love.

A string of many tears,
Stringed over the time,
Where no one will listen,
How the soul cries out, moans...

Love without soul love is a physical, carnal attraction, based on certain desires that are consumed, after the disappearance of the man's interest. It is only a passing state, without serious feelings and commitments, which brings great offense to the woman involved in such a relationship.The tears, the pain, the regrets, exist only in the heart of the one who has deluded himself, that just lovemaking is love.

Do you know what love is?
Feeling for a pleasure,
Which doesn't know what longing is,
The blood just screams, demands...

Lovemaking, it often happens for certain mutual favors, by which people are lured into the traps of momentary pleasure.

Let's make love my dear,
Only the stars in the sky to see us,
Afterwards please dear to forget me,
When I sit to waiting another spring...

People who do not want serious relationships or a family, they embrace the state of free and transient love as a carnal necessity, with people they do not want to tie their lives or feelings to.

Passing love…

The passing love can destroy relationships or families, turning the people's lives into an ordeal. Although at the beginning it breaks out as a passion for physical attraction, devoid of chosen feelings and hopes for the future, it can have a tragic end caused by one of the partners.

I thought you'd give me love,
But my dream was shattered,
You were a sweet delusion,
Which dragged my soul into sin...

Love has many faces and many names given by some and others, who only know how to pronounce this word, without knowing its true meaning and value.

What do you know what love is,
Weak man, at the mercy of chance?
Have you ever come across her,
To feel her, so you can forget her?

The forms of love are molded in the tender souls who liken it to blessedness, chosen feelings, and angelic bearing.

Love is earned...

Love is earned, through chosen behaviours, loyalty, simplicity, purity of soul, respect, kindness, attention, care, compassion, help. All these requirements are not easy to achieve, except for chosen souls people of integrity who know how to love and demonstrate through everything they do for that person.

Easy, to say words...

It's easy to say you love, as long as it's just some words that you hear repeated over and over, by the human robots who don't know what they're saying. First, love is loyal, it does not lie or deceive you no matter, how great the danger it is in. Who loves, loves till he dies, sacrifices till it dies and that person's words are always accompanied by deeds to prove, what it says.

Love is felt...

Do not believe in the words of love, which can lead you astray. Do not let your heart be warmed by these words alone, if the heart of the one who says it, is not warmed when it approaches to your heart. Love is felt in the human heart, then it goes to his mind where giving begins and spreads throughout the body, where good deeds of help, care, consideration, respect and loyalty begin to flow.

Carnal love, opposite to love...

Carnal love is part of love, but it comes at the same time with the feelings and never without them. Making love with someone you don't love, that is not a love but only a carnal attraction, a momentary wandering without importance and respect.

SINCERENESS

Sincerity is like a glass full of water, where the water is the sincerity, and the glass is the person who holds it.

Depending on how dirty the glass will be, so will the sincerity of the person.

Nowadays, sincerity is an anemia that everyone runs away from…

Yet, in this increasingly fake world, there are still honest people who are not loved, appreciated or supported.

It is certain that the remnants do not know how to appreciate sincerity...

Gossip and anger are the instruments of evil, with gossip are you preparing for the catafalque and the fury will pierce you.

I would like to say false words,
But my heart is crying,
That I don't know to play the pranks,
Also to act like anyone...

SOLIDARITY

Now I am in solidarity with you,
When I give to you my dream,
I forgot all about myself,
Just for cherish you...

Solidarity between two people is a divine connection, a lasting promise…

It is a relationship without tears and pain in the case of mutual love, the sharing of dreams and aspirations. And solidarity between friends or businesspeople, is the bond through which people help each other, collaborate and respect each other in the same way. But there is also the solidarity between politician's regardless of the parties they belong to, which get along well when they have common interests.

SUCCESS

I tell you to be successful in life,
And if we will meet,
I will change my mood,
To drink with you a glass of wine...

Success is represented by the laurels placed on the heads of the victors...

Sometimes, this success is well-deserved, coming after a very long period of hard work and dedication. That is why, honest people will always look to enjoy their own success with tears of joy. Instead, the plagiarists will triumph over the success snatched from the arms of fate, which put them in the right place and at the right time.

SUFFERING

To suffer alone on the earth,
When God has given you too much,
It is a stone from the grave,
Which presses on your forehead...

Suffering is a human state of mind, caused by someone or something…

In this regard, suffering collects many unspoken phrases, many reproaches held in the heart hidden, impenetrable thoughts, frustrations, worries and deep resentment not revealed to anyone.

If you suffer, it means you are alive...

Only people who suffer, know too well the definition of love, of sacrifice, dedication and care for other to be well. But there are and many people who experience suffering dramatically.

The solution to happiness is you don't associate with bad people…

The solution against to suffering lies within each human, to end suffering by solving problems positively. Resistance, waiver, confrontation, dialogue, are just some of the ways that can end suffering, because a person's suffering can have an unexpected end. Children have sufferings that they are afraid or ashamed to reveal to someone and finally end up making wrong decisions. Suffering cannot be controlled and is felt very deeply in the whole human being, but no one is forced to suffer.

Some suffer from everything nothing, and others die of thirst and the hunger...

That is why, all suffering should be end by positive actions, to help to lessen to protect the wounded heart and the attacked soul.

Bring spring into your life and the sun will rise again. The power lies only in the hand of the one who suffers and, in his will, to end this state, because to suffer alone for something or someone is like a suicide.

God gives to everyone only as much as he can carry…

When you've fallen, look to the sky in prayer, then, when you've overcome the difficulty, look to the sky once more and thank him.

Is anyone or anything worth any sacrifice?

The solution, wake up one morning like you haven't woken up in a long time. Take a deep breath and say done. No more suffering, compromises, words unsaid and held in the heart, collected thoughts, quarrels, hatred, discussions, humiliation, debasement, misunderstandings.

What is the point of all this in a relationship of any kind between people, if that relationship causes suffering?

Then think about drawing another map of your life, but where you make sure that nothing bad from what hurt comes through. Then you list the solutions to all your pains, and you will see that life is terribly beautiful. Leave everything behind you, because you are everything that needs to be saved, you are the voice that cries out in the wilderness of your heart. If you are not in good mood where you are or with whom you are, it means that you exist for nothing in that place. You cannot live if your being is always sad and should know that, in this world people mourn you only after you die.

Everyone wants something from you and uses you…

There are very few people who just want you to be around them. Who will hold your hand tightly, not to lose you and care of you with love when you are sick or helpless, proves that it is a precious person. You never to lose that person.

TOLERANCE

I don't know what you are and who you are,
You don't know anything of me either,
But don't try to hurt me,
Because I have nothing with you...

Tolerance is the most important word in the vocabulary of mankind, referring to the relationships and interaction between people.

Tolerance without limits, makes some think they are masters...

An important condition for tolerance not to turn into oppression, is that it is respected equally by all people. The moment a minority which has a certain lifestyle forces the majority to change its natural way of life, to become the same as that minority, then we are no longer talking about tolerance, but about the destruction of the human species, destruction of diversity and oppression.

So, let's think!

In a normal life cycle where people's lives are not destroyed and changed according to interests and politics, there exists tolerance and a natural coexistence. The people who have the power of decision in their hands, do not have to change the belief and the customs the normal in favour of the abnormal, just to subdue and manipulate the masses of people.

What God has given, let not human destroy...

When emancipation and progress permanently replace the past, then God is permanently removed from the equation. Either people cannot become gods, even if they act as if they were eternal gods. Countries with respect for humanity are very attentive to diversity, faith customs and human dignity, knowing that if something is imposed on a person upon without defending itself, then freedom has disappeared.

TRADITIONS

The traditions of the nation are part of the peaceful soul of the Romanian, from the distant times. Starting with working in the fields, folk dances in the villages, weddings and baptisms of children, funerals, festive meals, clothing, all had a place in the continuity of the Romanian being. We are a beautiful people, and we should stay that way. But when the traditions of a nation end up being a shame for those who disregard the past, then it is very clear that the nation's past is erased from the pages of history.

And what should a nation be proud of more than with those who raised the nation, from the difficult situation it was in through immeasurable sacrifices?

The emancipated claims that the high standard of life he leads, is due to him.

How come?

Can a baby bird just out of the nest, claim to have been born before the bird that feeds him with its own beak, so that it can finally be able to fly?

Some that are encouraged to come forward as any uneducated nullities, judge the past and history of a nation with tradition and help the indoctrination of future generations, who will not know the state of their nation's past is produced.

And why is the past stolen, thrown into the garbage dump, while a monstrosity of empty present, it is built without any truth or merit?

This question should grind each of us, if we still have a little of humanity and consideration for our great-grandparents. Humanity will sink deeper and deeper into the quagmire of troubles, being led by evil foolish debaucherous people without any definite goal and without faith in God, lovers of money and aggrandizement. When the humanity will be led by wise men, who will take the reins of power in politics and who will think when they control the destinies of the citizens, not just to rule like blind people, only then will we return to normality.

TRUST

Not to have trust,
Than only in God,
For he makes your life Heaven,
If you stand on his way...

Confidence is a precious wealth, which some people receive without knowing what to do with it.

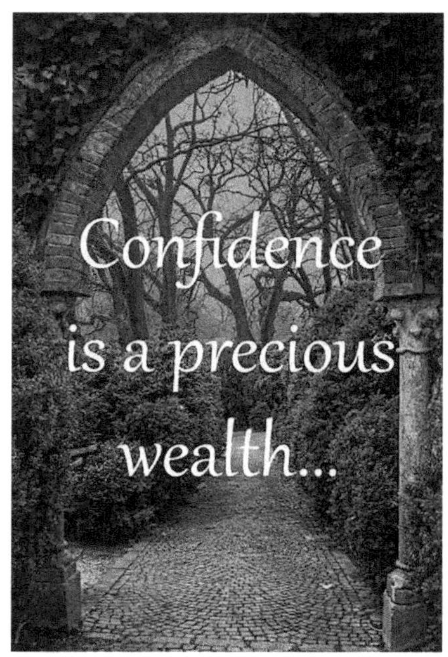

I trust you
And tell you what burns in my soul,
If I feel bad or if it is good,
I'm telling you, the man of God…

When the human get someone's trust, then that human becomes a brother to it and if it don't understand that thing, the loss will always be just on its side.

The soul of human is revealed by its deeds...

When you betray, you are followed by betrayal wherever you go, because what you give to others you will receive, that is how it is written in the order of nature. Traitors of any kind deserve no mercy, because they don't have mercy when they play with other people's lives.

Who values trust, holds the greatest wealth which will bear fruit, when it least expects it.

TRUTH

God, human and the earth, all these forms it taken together, form the truth.

Truth is not a definition with a destination, adaptable to the circumstances in which the interests are valued, where there are for and against groups, where a person is certain that it owns the truth, replacing the importance of the arguments. The truth is truth, it is a certainty which causes joy to some and brings damages to others. The truth discovered by each individual, is more credible than the truth presented by others.

What would be the truth?

Only by embracing the wisdom, can the truth be known to the extent that it can save an human.

If the truth is clearly seen by an ideologue, a name used by Napolean (1769-1821) who called his opponents "ideologues" or "salon doctrinaires", then surely we will have as arguments a lot of idealistic ethics, opinions and convictions; based on principles, the doctrines and symbols that define their existence in their well-defined groupings or interests.

On the other hand, the truth seen clearly by an idealist is directly based on honesty, creativity, emotions and promptness; in solving problems in their real form in which they are at the time, looking for real ideas and solutions without giving attention to the words, betting more on the chances of changing the situation and giving it a precise form.

How is truth seen?

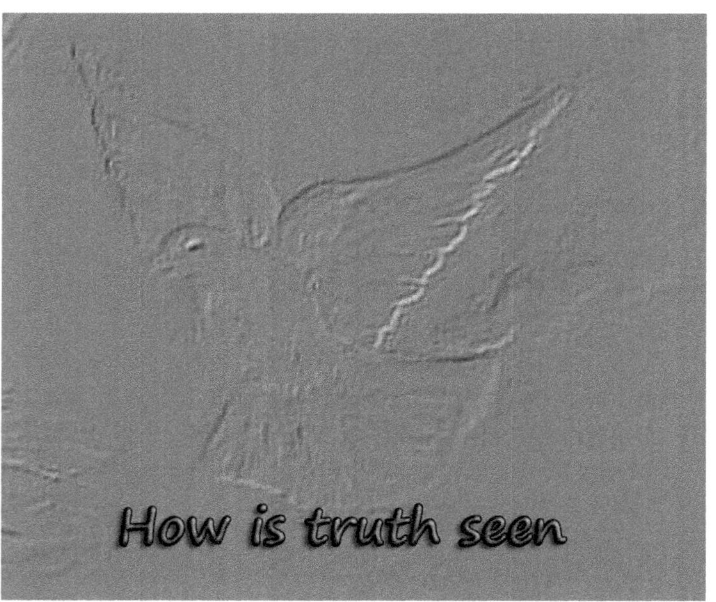

The truth is seen as a sword that stands permanently over the head of the guilty or the debtor and as a deliverance to the one who waits for justice to be done.

The master of truth...

As is well known, it is truth that rules us and no human on earth can call himself the master of the truth. The truth is perceived and seen differently by each person. Often the truth is in the wrong hands and finding it depends on the wisdom, character, education and vision of the one who is put to find out the truth and do the justice. Therefore, for these reasons we observe that after the "resolution" of a dispute, the party that lost the case says that it was not served justice. Even if man had the right arguments for finding out the truth, it was ignored. That attitude was taken only because of interests that would have been injured, if the truth had taken its rightful place and the justice had been done.

Die with the truth in your hand...

Sometimes it happens that people are wronged, especially when they are oppressed, unfairly blamed or simply ignored because of some vested interests; by those who punish their victims using unjust methods, attacks and destruction. That's why regardless of the age, the wronged, abused and ignored person remains a person marked for life, because the justice was not done at the right time; because the truth was truncated, denied or even made to appear absent. The most serious is the case where a child was wronged from an early age and the wrong was not corrected at the right time. That child will grow up mentally damaged, becoming a person who will hate the truth and the justice, because he was not given justice when he was abused. And no matter how much false happiness may show someone who was abused in his childhood, when it is alone in the private live, feels frustrated and wronged because of the period of childhood persecution.

With tears the soul was accompanied, the words to hide them...

There are many cases of famous people who have revealed their lives, and some of their lives were destroyed by the memories and wounds of the past that was not treated in time.

The truth in couple relationships...

If we refer to the truth within a couple relationship, then we can say that we see around us more and more people who are carried out in every way and who lack nothing, but who are not happy and fulfilled, ultimately failing in those relationships. And because of problems some of them turn into different people than the others knew them, sometimes they even becoming evil and vengeful due to the accumulation of hatred after the many years of restraint. That period when they posed as good people, smiling, very helpful, open to everything, accepting everything, they being involved in all good or bad ideas, not judging the bad deed of anyone who showed harmful behaviour, truncating the truth and always according with their own interest.

The masked people...

Usually, this type of people are the people who wear the invisible mask, the one that misleads you. They are very agreeable in any society, all doors are opened to them being named pleasant people, because they never contradict the sociable people, those who might turn their backs on them. These people know how to make themselves pleasant in society, but they have a hidden and harmful behavior for those which live next to them, turning them into their victims. Also, they lead a double life in relationships, always having someone which they hold close. They keep their lives separate,and hidden from the eyes of their partners who do not have access to their lives plans and peculiarities. Always they keep in touch with partners from previous relationships, posing as good people with the idea of changing the minds of those they broke up with and with the goal of making them regret breaking up with them. In most cases, their lives are based on lie and at the slightest dispute they are ready to get rid of the present victim, for to bring back a victim from the past or a new victim. Being unstable, they do not get involved in relationships and give only the minimum in everything being stingy with their partners and very generous with others. In addition, they do not make future plans and do not discuss with their partners being cold and distant, having only a robotic and repetitive behavior of daily tasks. That is why they often spend years in a relationship without loving their partners, touching them, showing them consideration, love, attention, but simply tormenting them and trying to drive them away when don't want they anymore.

They know how to fool...

They also, like to flirt anywhere and with anyone, manipulating the partners on the face without hiding. Showing them that they don't care if they hurt them, without shame, with a lot of indifference and without any regret or gratitude for those who lose the meaning of life by living with them. And if the partners dare to protest, then they are blamed for their behavior, are lied to and erronate confronted even as they experience betrayal and see the truth truncated in front of them. They fool you to your face by showing your weakness, when you are a helpless person. Often, as the saying goes, one's word against another, is more important than the truth at face value. Here the truth can also depend on the audience which is almost always on the side of the deceiver, categorizing his betrayal as unjustified jealousy on the part of the partner, the one who observes and experiences the moments of betrayal. While they see the flirtations just as friendly and innocent as socializing. These people with false masks accusing their partners of exaggerating calling them liars, jealous, evil, turning their partners into frustrated and wronged victims, who in turn will not be able to recover from such relationships for a long time.

The truth about deceivers, in relations with others...

Some of these deceivers behave injuriously towards people who seek the justice, love honor and are malleable, using on them when they want. They can even go so far, as to copy the appearance of those that they hate and envy, dressing like them, imitating them in everything and seducing the partners. Regardless of age and occupation, they are usually below the level of the person they are attacking, they do their best to appear attractive to the partners of those they are attacking them with the intention of causing breakups, humiliation and even public aggression. There are such cases everywhere of people who do not feel good with themselves or with others being always unstable and looking for new victims, hating the truth and the justice because they have no value as human beings. It is very harmful to live around people with false masks, because they destroy you rapidly from the inside. These people can destroy the human dignity, to turn you into a sad, frustrated and dissatisfied person who cannot love life and live in peace. No matter how close you are to such people, the solution to avoid suffering is to stay as far away from them as possible. Because these people know how to trap anyone in their trap with great ease; because they have the capacity to harm and manipulate; they destroying out of envy, malice or interest. The most correct thing would be for them to receive that they give to others, by experiencing the suffering and to think carefully when they want to torture someone. There would be a lot to say about these characters who torment people and they are like stones around the necks of those who are unlucky enough to encounter them.

The wolf changes its hair, but its temper not...

Bad character never changes, especially in old age. And no matter how much a person hides its nature, in the end it will be revealed because time reveals everything and the masks will fall of their own accord.

Solutions for the truth...

Justice next to truth looks good, but justice next to power is far from the truth. When there is a problem, the solution need to be found to solve it directly, without distortions and scenarios about truth presented by some, just based only on the facts evaluated correctly. But this cause requires a lot of patience, trust in the one who evaluates the problem and perseverance when it doesn't happen to be solved immediately. The patient and persevering person, will find the solution to all problems that will arise during its life.

What do you do when the truth disappears?

No matter how much, a human is wronged when the truth is on his side, it can find a way out of the situation that worries it. That human makes peace with itself, does not blame itself for what happened, does not make assumptions or scenarios, but deals with the problem. It tries to judge the problem coldly, seeing it exactly as it was, without doing justice to itself, treats it as if it had happened to someone else and he is the observer, who should see the solution without delay. Because the problem seen from the outside, presents a clearer vision than that of the actual included participant, who sees justice on his side. If the problem is not solved, then it looks for help around, someone who will strengthen and support him to move more easily to solving the problem. If that help exists, immediately accepts it. If there is no one to help him, the human tries to solve the problem itself. By breaking away from that situation, leaves it behind as a great pain, but which must end as soon as possible, so as not to cause more suffering. It is necessary that everything boils down to an unpleasant memory and an ugly experience, which should be left where they were and happened. To be a buried secret and not to be talked about it with anyone. The transformation of evil into a past that need never be remembered, the help, love, compassion, courage, forgetting, all these bring forgiveness and survival of person, who can adapt to any situation.

Knock and it will be opened to you...

Faithful people usually turn to priests and at divinity having the faith that things will work out in the end, they come to terms with the situation more easily solving things calmly and knowing that there is someone who solves everything. There are also cases where people seek for qualified help, but it does not help too much some. Not all people are the same from a mental point of view, feelings, experiences and for these reasons not all diagnoses give the same result, following the applied treatments. Therefore, some end up using the solutions which can help them forget temporary. But with time they become dependent on the methods used for the moment, ending up experiencing a much bigger disaster and even resorting to regrettable acts.There is always a solution, if the problem is solved immediately and if there is someone who cares, geting involved and helps. People are not alone, unless they want to be alone and isolate themselves from the rest of the world. The loneliness sickens the soul, body and brain, bringing all kinds of diseases, turning someone into a pessimistic, grumpy and sick person. We also know that any human exists on earth to be happy, to have healthy relationships with those around it, to start a family, with the goal of not living alone. People are free to live as their conscience dictates, education and will to enjoy life freely.

VALUES

The riches of a country, defend the future of descendants the country...

Values can be the material, human, fundamental and moral wealth.

Material values...

Our country as a gate,
It opens to share,
All we have in our little heaven,
To the grabbing and evil strangers...

Human values...

Our historian Mircea Eliade (1907-1986) said about our nation's poet Mihai Eminescu (1850-1889), that "if the Romanian people disappear from the face of the earth and a book by Eminescu remains, the world will know who the Romanians were..."

Poets, writers, painters, composers, artists, geniuses, sculptors and all those full of talent are incomparable human values, blessed with the talent and skills which should be protected by the society in which they live.

Their disappearance impoverishes the world and the countries...

What the school looks like today, that's what Romania's future will look like tomorrow. If we have a society that does not know how to protect and love the values of the nation given by God as our wealth, then we are a nation destined for destruction. Because today's society is full of people without any merits, wich are usually envious, hold grudges against the merits of others, thwarting them plans unjustly.

Fundamental values...

These values define the quality of a nation's and through freedom, truth, justice, beauty, we can step head up, into the world around us. When a country's fundamental values are at risk, then vigilance is the beacon that must light unceasingly.

Moral values...

If God didn't exist, then there wouldn't even be love...

The values are the golden laurels placed on the head of the one who guards faith, respect, purity of soul, sincerity, truth, loyalty, kindness, normality, justice.

Disunity is good sister to failure...

A lie of any kind is a lie, and depravity lead to disorder and chaos. We have too few quality people and too many worthless people. When the abnormal is applauded as normal, then the end of civilization has begun because this earth has become like a cesspool, in which many soil themselves without knowing what they are doing, or they do it because that is what the crowd does. And to be different from the crowd means to be a disagreeable human, disinherited from earthly gifts. And are too many without wisdom which can make an idol out of an executioner. That's why, many fall as low as possible and only a few manage to get up. But it is known that the master of all things, will straighten them all out at the right time.

WICKEDNESS

Evil is the opposite of good...

Human judgment should come from above from the heaven, because there is God; that is justice, love, the holy beauty, the clouds that disperse so that the sun can come out and illuminate us. While the judgment that comes from below, is from the earth from people, from those who have no right to judge others. Because if we look down to the ground, we see people with hatred, malice, envy, defamation, teasing and vain struggles for nothing.

Then why should someone judge you who doesn't have pure feelings for you; doesn't give you anything never; doesn't do anything for you; doesn't know your heart, your hardships, your joys, your feelings?

What right does such a human have to talk about you, to dare to disturb you and attack your existence without causing it any inconvenience?

A human should take care of its own and when there are no worthy people around to accompany it, to fill its time with other joys than complicating its life with people who saddens its mind and the heart with vain things.

Loose mouth should be stopped when it attacks...

Also, the blow received from behind by words can be fatal, because you can't hear that enemy to face him, and when someone verbally attacks you it disturbs your soul and that's when self-defence occurs.

A humans hatred is stronger than a sword...

This means that you either get into the mind of the unwise human and answer him the inevitable occurring or you turn your back on him and ignore him. If you put yourself at the mind of an unwise man you might lose a lot, first you spoil your good mood, nerves affect your health and quarrels lead to complications, beatings, swearing, a mixed vocabulary with everything.

Does man need all these problems which coming from the unwise man, who does not know how to refrain and does not see his own?

Ignoring the unwise man changes your mood a bit, you're momentarily annoyed that you can't teach him a lesson but ignoring him brings you less trouble.

Is it worth giving the unwise the satisfaction of feeling important, that you let him into your life?

It doesn't deserve and being ignored by everyone, in the end will see only of its life. It depends on how much this insistence of the unwise, who wants to make your life hell at all costs, affects you. Silence and the distance are the weapons against the unwise. Wickedness has always been like a trap attached to some, who got hold of the dignity and patience of good characters. Unfortunately, wickedness has no cure, the wicked person should be left in his wickedness. Weed grows randomly, doesn't whether it is loved or hated. She doesn't care how much mess she makes around her, she grows and becomes more and more visible. It is important that to stop at the time, so that it does not expand. A bad man is a bad man, and no one can put kindness in his heart. Being a good man, if by chance you have wronged you apologize, to exonerate yourself, to tie the thread where it was broken, because you are sorry and want to set things right. But you come across someone who offends you and knocks you down like a tree in all its glory, telling you words you didn't believe that you can ever hear them. Worse, you are wronged, and you protest explaining to human that you feel wronged, but the human continues to blame you for its behaviour and insults as well.

And then, why give pearls to swine?

The solution would be to run away from that human and not let to affect you too much, because what you needed to know you found out. Not all those who call themselves friends are friends, not all those who come from the same family are relatives, those who cause you problems and sadness are not people. People with dignity will keep their right place in their lives, will judge their deeds and correct themselves when needed. Otherwise, all those who are not human we can call them weeds, that grow where they are not allowed and bind themselves to what should not be their personal problem. Evil people who discourage you and convince you that you are not capable, do not know what humanity means, and cannot even be considered a Christian fellowship for anyone. That's why it's good not to let anyone hurt you, because wounds don't go away easily. Anyone who doesn't respect you isn't worth wasting your time on, better to go in your own way. Whoever watches how you cry without hugging you, has no heart for you. Whoever falls asleep peacefully after an argument with you, is the man who doesn't care that you exist and can't wait for you to leave. He who does not talk to you and holds grudges, behaves as if he were made of ice, is the human of displeasure who will bring you many troubles. The solution is to run as far as possible from people who are not smiling, are not happy, are not peacemaker, who day by day have same words and behaviours of cold people, they don't know how to laugh, they don't enjoy with you for everything and having nothing to share with you.

Historian Nicolae Iorga (1871 – 1940) said that "The soul is like iron. You can't work with him until you warmed him up. "

WISDOM

The wisdom of an old human it is the people's wealth
and who does not have a wise man, to buy him...

Where there is wisdom there is everything, tranquility, peace, blessing, beauty, temperance, respect, kindness, honesty, truth, fairness, compassion, divinity, abundance. Also, the country ruled by the wise, competent, honest, frugal, loyal, fair people, is seen from afar as a strong fortress, decorated for the celebration. And the house where wise people live is always beautified with tranquility, peace, joy, abundance, acceptance, love, forgiveness, temperance, has always blooming flowers and smells of warm bread. In this world are people that you always want them to be around, from whom you have a lot to learn, some you would like to see from time to time and some people you never want to see. The wise man inclines to earthly conduct with great care, for heaven shall be his cradle and the earth shall be, the resting place of his bones. Wisdom teaches you to be human, because to be human is to be just, good, fair, content, forgiving and grateful.

A wise man is a wealth, in a woman's house...

The wisdom of the woman rests a lot on the shoulder of the wise man, because if the woman has a wise man, he will know how to guide his woman.

WOMAN

The woman is as a poem, seen with her soft eyes as an icon of gentleness and beauty, how she caresses her baby while he is sleeping at her warm breast. And her face blossoms, when the man she loves gives her a kiss, and her heart sings all the songs of love when she is told that she is loved. She is the divine being, sung and adored by all poets.

Woman kissed by the sun's rays, I caress you in thought and in poetry...

She is full of love, beauty, tenderness and candour, through which life descends shyly to earth. So, nothing can replace the woman, no matter how much someone tries to clone her, imitate her, dethrone her from her place, rightfully given by the heavenly divinity.

The woman has expectations from a relationship...

That's why, when a woman enters a relationship, she expects a love that will last, wants appreciation and respect, dedication to the point of sacrifice, stability to the point of death, special attention, soulful compassion, help from her beloved, understanding and a blessed patience. But above all these, the woman expects a continuity of the strong feelings and the identical behaviour with the period in which she was courted.

Why does a woman expect all this from a man?

Because she is the first who bestows on the man, all these gifts of their love and total dedication to the ultimate sacrifice. For this reason, she expects to receive all that she gives, the immeasurable riches of the human soul.

But, if the man changes, he doesn't have a continuation of the feelings and behaviour of the period when woman was courted, then and woman changes as the man shapes her. Depending on how a woman receives from a man, she returns in the same way all the care and promises he made to her, when he convinced her to enter his life.

The woman is the mirror of the man and when the man disregards her, he is disregarded.

When a man demeans his wife in front of another woman by comparing and wounding her, he shows his weak character and is quick to open the path of hatred to his wife's heart. And when the man does not take care of his wife then himself prepares the hard times for the time when she will have to take care of him, show him love, attention and consideration. Everything that the man gives to his wife, he will also receive in return from her, depends on how much he disappointed her, because a good woman will always find her place.

A good woman is a rarity, in our days...

Now, when femininity has its full say and woman's independence can easily replace any man who has become loveless and careless it is very unwise, to leave a loving woman for any fleeting relationship, you may dream of. Because the woman knows how to always receive and give to the one who deserves it, a beautiful life. And to him who does not deserve to be called a man, the woman lets him destroy himself and then leaves him. A strong woman is always the treasure of the family, because she carries every problem and every family burden without getting tired.

The man's behavior alienates the woman...

But she will leave the relationship when the man cheats on her, humiliates her in front of another woman, betrays her on her face and makes her to leave.

A real woman who respects herself, doesn't destroy another woman's house...

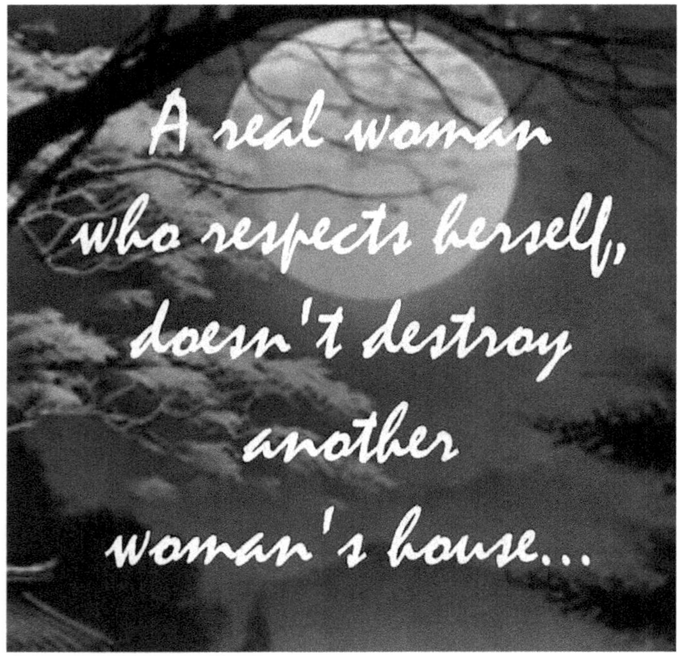

Women with dignity, do not allow themselves to be humiliated by the reckless betrayals and the vile gestures made to shameless women by the ridiculous men.They fight for their relationship and if men don't want them anymore, then they leave.

WORRY

Worries are left at home,
If you go to face it,
With a better life,
Without to insult the mind...

Everyone worries about any failure, but this kills the idea in its infancy start, without giving it a chance to be born. Grandfathers used to say that when you go to battle, go bravely and without worrying about the outcome. If you don't get out of bed to face the problem, then you're not going to succeed.

If you don't knock, how do you want to be answered?

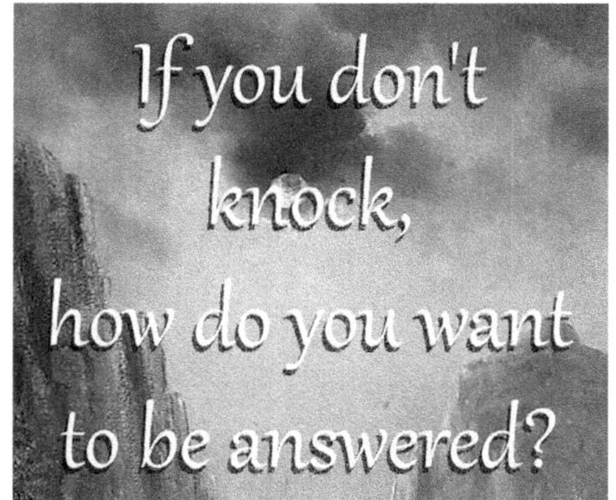

Action is what decides which side you will be on, and courage gives you the dignity to defend yourself. Human should not judge others without reason, only if it was offended or wronged. Care comes from a sense of responsibility, on the other hand often a parent who feels responsible for its children, gives them everything it has and that is not bad. But it should give where there is absolutely needed at that moment, because to encourage laziness and avarice is not good care, but rather a recklessness.

Care has its role...

Caring for people is a biblical requirement, it is a requirement of humanity and kindness to be used sparingly where it is really needed, not where there is manipulation and ulterior motives. In the past, caring for people was rewarded, appreciated and blessed, because people were closer to God. In these times, caring for people is interpreted, judged and rewarded with bad deeds many times. Man should first take care of itself, the person it lives with and of those who visit it to enjoy together. To lay a shoulder where there is trouble and a kind word where there is pain, this means a charity.

YOUTH

Youth, rare flower,
You pass like a springtime,
I am waiting and still hoping,
A power from the high heaven...

Youth without old age and life without death, cannot exist. Only in the fairy tales our grandparents told us at bedtime, there was youth without old age. Normally, all people are young for a while, then they turn into old people as the years go by. Because eternal youth does not mean the beauty of the face changed in aesthetic operations and other artificial beautification procedures. These are only some ways to slow down, but no definitive solutions. What belongs to youth and a person must not lose in this life, is honesty, the courage to fight by the spirit of justice and freedom, the audacity to act when life requires it. Other values of youth are big dreams and their fulfilment, the bravery, respect and consideration for those around you, humanity, compassion, love, family, friendships, opportunities, aspirations, ideals, desires, love and character chosen. Youth depend on the strength and health of the body, which should not be abused and used in inappropriate transformations. All these are the values of the young person, only its and which remain as a dowry for its whole life. Our ancestors were proud of all that was Romanian.

About the author

Stefania Rotariu was born on December 27, 1963, in Sucevita, Suceava county, Romania. She spent part of her childhood in the beautiful Bucovina, where the seed of inspiration was planted. She began writing poems at an early age, collecting them over the years. The poems, written on notebooks, were later rewritten on an old typewriter and bound, keeping them until publication. She attends the University of Law in Timisoara, Romania, but withdraws in her last year of studies, heading towards a career in the IT field, in which she dedicates herself until 2007, when she leaves Romania and heads to Spain, where she lives 3 years. She returns to Romania in the spring of 2010 and stays until the end of the year, leaving Romania again to settle in England. There she takes university courses to work as telecommunications engineer, after which she takes further university courses to specialize in cyber security. The abroad brings her satisfaction and the money needed for publish the books she has written and prepared for printing. Life away from the country and her loved ones, made her stronger in decision-making, to know how to carve out a life in which her dreams come true. But as nothing is achieved without sacrifice, her health has deteriorated over the years, making her less active. So, in the rest of the time that life offers her, she decided to translate all 5 volumes of poems from Romanian into English, published until 2024. In addition, she published in 2024 the books: "CUGETARI" in Romanian and "MEDITATIONS" in English.

Editorial debut

Publication of the first volume of poems: "POEZII PENTRU INIMA TA" (POEMS FOR YOUR HEART) in the summer of 2012 (America) in Romanian language; volumes II, III of poems published in the summer of 2014 (England); volumes IV, V of poems published in February 2023 (England); "CUGETARI", a book published in the summer of 2024 (England) in Romanian language and "MEDITATIONS", a book published in English, in the summer of 2024. She dedicates herself to cultural life and becomes a member of the Writers' Union of England in 2012, in 2017 she becomes a British journalist and in 2020 she international journalist. Worked for one year with FRP TV as moderator and producer of the show "În Căutarea Adevărului" (In Search of the Truth), continuing with journalistic work. Participates at the International Festival of Poetry and Epigram (Romeo and Juliet at Mizil) and the Anthological Poetry Collection (With the Country in the Soul - for love, mourning and longing) in Romania. She collaborates with different soloists by putting her lyrics to music, then shared on YouTube.

Friendship is a wonderful gift.
For you, my dear friend.
Stefania Rotariu

Stefania Rotariu
Life is a joy, if you know how to get the best out of it.
Beauty is a gift from God, if you know how to value it.
Love cannot be described in words, it can only be felt.
Friendship is the most beautiful gift you can give to a person.
Your smile can cheer up a sad and downcast heart.
Your sacrifice can save a hopeless life.

www.ingramcontent.com/pod-product-compliance
Lightning Source LLC
Chambersburg PA
CBHW040536170726
48295CB00012B/489

* 9 7 8 1 9 1 5 3 5 1 2 9 6 *